Drawing and Sketching

Deri Robins

MINNETONKA, MINNESOTA

This edition published in 2006 in North America by
Two-Can Publishing
11571 K-Tel Drive
Minnetonka, MN 55343
www.two-canpublishing.com

Two-Can wishes to thank artist Shannon Steven for
her help with the American terms in this book.

Library of Congress CIP data on file

ISBN 1-58728-543-6

Written by Deri Robbins
Designed by Wladek Szechter/Louise Morley
Edited by Sian Morgan/Matthew Harvey
Illustrated by Melanie Grimshaw

Creative Director: Louise Morley
Editorial Manager: Jean Coppendale

Credits
Corbis Rune Hellestad p15
Jean Coppendale p26, p28

Printed and bound in China

1 2 3 4 5 10 09 08 07 06

The words in **bold** are
explained in the glossary
on page 30.

Contents

Getting started

Anyone can draw—it's just a matter of learning how to look at the world around you! This book has lots of techniques to help you improve your drawings.

colored pencils

To get started, you'll need a pad of paper, a couple of pencils, an eraser, and a pencil sharpener. As you learn more, you may want to try some of the other materials described below.

Pencils

You need at least three types of pencils: 2H (a hard pencil, for sharp lines and details); HB (medium-hard, for sketching), and 2B (a soft pencil, for drawing guidelines and for **shading**.) 4B to 8B pencils are very soft, and are for dark shading.

Eraser

Not just for deleting! You can use it to make **highlights** in your drawings by revealing the paper underneath.

Charcoal and chalk

Charcoal and **chalk** are great for making quick sketches, filling in large areas of color, and adding **texture**.

Oil or chalk pastels

Chalk pastels are soft and crumbly. They give a delicate, blurry effect when you smudge them. Oil pastels make brighter colors.

Pens and felt-tips

These are perfect for strong black lines or sharp detail. You'll need some with thick points, and some with thinner ones.

Wax crayons

Cheap and good for making bold, colorful pictures.

Paper

Use lots of different types, sizes, and colors of paper. You can make your own cheap sketchpads by stapling scrap paper together. Save your best paper for your final drawings. Experiment with different textures of paper. Smooth **sketch paper** is best for pencil and pen drawings. The rough surface of **construction paper** is ideal for pastels, chalk, crayons, and charcoal. The marks on the paper will look different depending on the kind of paper you use.

chalk

crayons

pastels

pencils

eraser

art paper

Get inspired!

You can find inspiration for your drawing projects wherever you look. Carry a small sketchbook with you wherever you go, so that you can jot down ideas and make quick, on-the-spot sketches. You can turn these into finished pictures later on.

When you find an interesting object to draw, make a sketch and note its color and texture—it might be smooth, rough, or bumpy.

Become an art collector

Collect interesting materials to help you with your drawings. Your collection might include leaves, colored scraps of paper, patterns, photos, stamps, labels, and pictures from newspapers and magazines. Paste them into a scrapbook or file them away neatly in a large box. Empty cereal boxes make good art files.

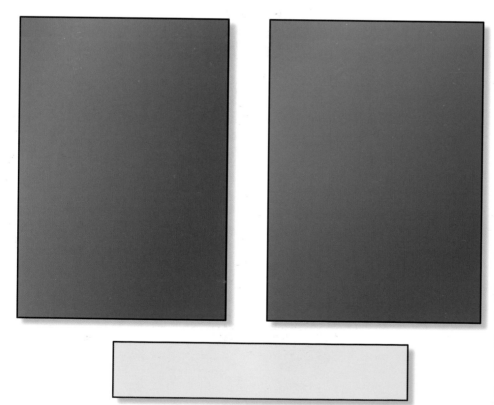

Store your finished drawings safely in a **portfolio**—a large, stiff folder that will keep your drawings flat. You can make one from cardboard or thick paper.

1 You'll need two pieces of cardboard, a strip of fabric, some strong tape or glue, and some string or ribbon.

2 Place the two pieces of cardboard opposite each other. Glue the fabric securely to the two pieces of cardboard. Make a hole in the outer edge of piece of cardboard as shown.

glue the fabric to the two pieces of cardboard

3 Let the glue dry, then loop string or ribbon through the holes at the top of the portfolio. Tie them securely so that your art will be safe. Finally, add decoration to the outside of your portfolio to make it look more interesting.

Color and shading

Filling in a drawing with solid blocks of color gives it a bold, dramatic look, but also tends to make objects look flat. If you want your picture to look more three-dimensional, you need to add shading.

Hatching

This is how most artists add shade and texture to their drawings. You can make areas darker just by adding more lines. Try these techniques.

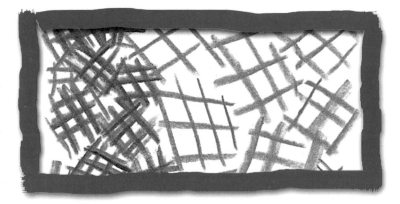

1 In crosshatching, you draw two sets of lines running across each other.

2 Curved hatching lines are good for making shapes look round.

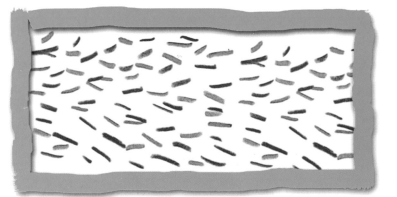

3 Use short lines for drawing fur or feathers. Experiment with pens and pencils.

4 The more lines you draw, the darker the shade.

Scribble shading
Small scribbles are good for fast, energetic-looking sketches, such as this one of a guinea pig.

Smudging
Smudging soft pencil, pastel, or charcoal lines gives a soft shading effect.

Making highlights
Use an eraser to delete parts of the shading and make highlights. This can create pools of light or make parts of the picture look shiny.

Dot shading
Closely drawn dots give soft shading to a picture. Try using more than one color. Then look at the picture from a distance and see how the dots blend.

Self-portrait

One of the best ways to learn how to sketch people's faces is to draw pictures of yourself. First sketch a quick self-portrait from memory on scrap paper.

Perfect portraits

Is your face round, oval, heart-shaped, or square? If you can't tell, use a soft pencil or crayon and trace the shape of your face on a mirror. Then look at the outline and see what shape it is.

Next, think about your features. What shape are your eyes? Are your lips thin or full? Is your nose long or short?

Now, look carefully at your reflection as you follow the steps on page 11. Think about the shading and texture as well as shape and position of your features.

Compare it with the first sketch you did. You'll be amazed how much better your new drawing is!

Follow these steps to help you get all your features in the right place:

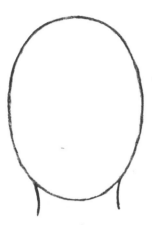

1 Think about the shape of your face. Use a soft pencil to sketch the **outline**.

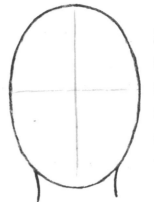

2 Draw a line down the middle of the face, and another one just above the center from side to side.

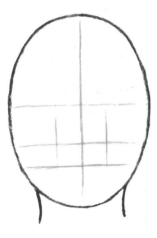

3 Now divide the lower half into two. Then draw three more lines: one **horizontal** and two **vertical**, as shown here.

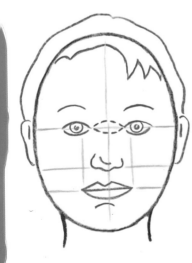

4 Use the lines as a guide to sketch in your eyes. Leave one eye width between them. For your mouth, start with the line between the lips, then add the outline of the upper and lower lips. Draw in the tip of your nose, but not the sides.

5 Add your ears, hair, eyelashes, eyebrows, chin, and other details. Switch to colored pencils and use shading to define the curves. Fill in with color.

Drawing faces

When you feel confident about drawing your own portrait, try drawing other people. Faces come in all shapes and sizes, and everyone's features are different. You can create hundreds of different faces by making an Identikit set.

Identikit set

1 Draw four or five different face outlines, all the same size. Divide each into three sections.

2 Now cut lots of strips of paper, each the same width as the sections of the faces.

3 Draw different-shaped eyes on some of the strips, noses on others, and mouths on the rest, all with different expressions.

4 Now mix and match the features on the different faces. You can cut out hairlines, mustaches, and glasses, too.

5 When you've created a face you like, trace or copy the outline and features onto another piece of paper. Use colored pencils to turn it into a finished drawing.

EGG HEADS

It's not quite as easy to draw people's faces from the side, or from above or below! A hard-boiled egg can be a very useful tool for practicing.

1   **2**   **3**

1   Draw 4 lines on the egg exactly as shown.

2   Draw in the features. Stick a blob of clay on for the nose.

3   Using your egg-head as a model, practice drawing the face from different angles.

ART FILE

People don't smile all the time! Collect photos and newspaper cuttings of faces with different expressions, and practice drawing them.

Drawing people

The easiest way to draw figures is to think about the parts of the body as simple shapes. For example, think of the head as an egg shape, and the arms and legs as sausages or tubes.

1 Start with the head at the top of your paper. Draw an egg shape.

2 Add a short tube for the neck. It should be almost as wide as the head.

3 Now draw an oval for the top of the body.

4 Draw the arms as if they were two sausage shapes with a circle in the middle.

5 Draw the rest of the torso using ovals and circles.

6 Draw the legs in the same way as the arms, but make them wider at the top.

7 Finally, add simple hand and foot shapes. Now draw a line around the outside of this mass of shapes. This is the outline of your figure.

Now use the same steps to draw figures sitting, lying down, or crawling. Look at people in different poses or from different angles to get some ideas.

TRY THIS

Sketch your shapes roughly at first. Draw lightly with a soft pencil. When you're happy with the basic figure, then move on to the details. Erase the original lines when you're done.

Make a poster

Find some photos of your favorite athlete, movie star, or musician, and draw him or her by building up from simple shapes.

Use different pens, pencils, and crayons for your picture. What different effects can you create? Remember to use shading for the dark areas and leave highlights for the light areas.

SOCCER

Figures in motion

How can you make figures look as if they are really moving? A number of simple techniques will help you bring your sketches to life.

Art in action

Choose a photograph of someone moving. Make a quick sketch of the figure, using loose strokes. Use your whole arm and not just your fingers and wrist. Try to look at the figure—not at what you are drawing!

Keep your pencil moving all the time, hardly lifting it from the paper. Draw sweeping lines that follow the direction of the motion. This will help give the appearance of speed and movement, and make your figure look more realistic.

TIP

Take your sketchbook to an event where there will be lots of movement, such as a baseball game, a gymnastics meet, or a dance performance. Make quick sketches of the figures as you watch. Or, record an event on TV and play it back. Pause it when you see something you want to draw.

Practice drawing action shots of athletes or dancers. Use colored pencils to make bold scribble drawings. Leave out the details and just focus on what they are doing.

These movement sketches can be helpful later on, when you are drawing a more polished picture.

TIP

Adding "speed lines" really brings your action figures to life! Curved lines make your figures look as if they are twirling around. Straight lines make your figures look as if they are speeding by!

Perfect pets

Just as human figures can be made up of "eggs and sausages" (page 14), you can draw great pictures of pets by combining simple shapes.

Cat

You can draw a cat from three simple circles.

1 Using a soft pencil, lightly sketch three circles, two for the body and one for the head. Make the head smaller than the body. Add the ears, front legs, and the curl of the tail.

2 Use colored pencils to complete the outline of the cat. You can now erase any lines you don't need.

3 Now draw in the details: eyes, whiskers, fur, and markings.

1

2

3

Here are some other animals for you to sketch.

SCRAPBOOK

Collect photos and drawings of as many animals as you can find, including your pets or a pet that you would like to have. Great pictures can be found on stamps, greeting cards, magazines, and websites.

TIP

Try drawing different types of cats and dogs from photos you've collected—or from real life, if they will sit still long enough! Remember that heads, tails, ears, and fur are never the same from animal to animal.

Fur and feathers

Sketching the outline is only the first step when drawing animals. To really bring your drawings to life, you need to add texture. One way to do this is to make different types of markings with colored pencils.

Dogs and cats
Use soft pencils to scribble a curly coat, or to draw a fluffy tail.

Reptiles
Snakes; lizards, and turtles have interesting geometric patterns and markings.

Fish
Lots of little curved lines are ideal for the scales of a fish.

Birds
Use a hard pencil to draw long, straight lines for the tail feathers, and short, curvy lines for the shorter feathers of the head and chest.

Experiment with different art materials to see which ones produce the most realistic effects for your animals.

Try drawing the same animal using different materials. What happens? How are they different?

Soft pencils or charcoal give a wider, softer effect, and are perfect for drawing fluffy animals.

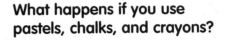

What happens if you use pastels, chalks, and crayons?

Hard pencils make thin, light lines— great for showing off this squirrel's fluffy tail.

Pens and markers make strong, black lines. The finer the point, the thinner the lines.

Landscapes

When it comes to drawing a **landscape**, how do you decide which details to put in, and which to leave out? Making a viewfinder can help you make up your mind.

Make a viewfinder

A viewfinder is a frame with a hole in the middle. Make it out of two L-shaped pieces of cardboard. This will allow you to change the shape to make a square or a rectangle.

1 Cut an L-shape out of cardboard. Trace around it to make an identical shape, and cut this one out, too.

2 Use paperclips to hold the ends together in the shape of a rectangle.

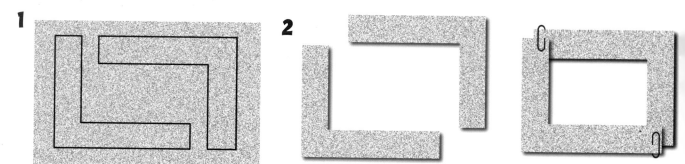

TIP

Silhouettes are solid, **dark** outlines of objects, in which you can't see any details such as color and texture. Use a black pen or marker to draw dramatic silhouettes of trees in **a winter landscape** or at sunset. The trees really stand out!

Using the viewfinder

1 Hold the viewfinder in front of you. Look through the hole as if it were a camera lens. Make the hole smaller or larger. Move the viewfinder around until you find a view you like. Check the view both horizontally and vertically.

2 When you have chosen your view, quickly sketch the main parts of the picture with a soft pencil (you can erase it afterward) using one hand. This is your rough outline for the finished picture to indicate large areas, such as grass, sky, or water. Sketch in the position of any buildings or trees.

3 When you have done the outlines, put the viewfinder away and finish the picture, filling in the details using colored pencils, chalks, or pastels.

Looking at trees

A tree can be an interesting object to draw. As with any subject, look carefully at it before you start to draw. Notice how branches grow out of other branches, rather than all coming straight from the trunk.

There are a huge variety of tree shapes.

Some trees have long branches that reach out to the side.

Some trees are are very tall and thin.

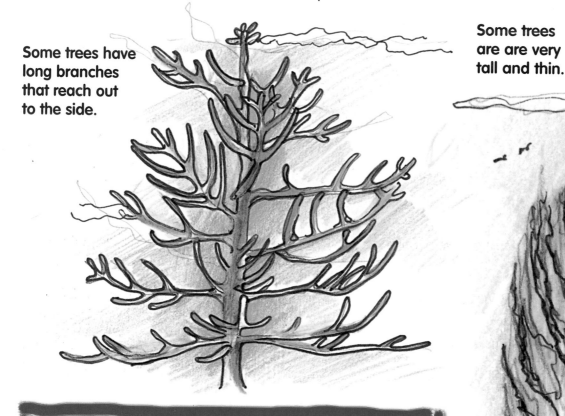

UP CLOSE

Bark varies a lot, too. Rubbings are a great way to collect different types of bark for reference. Put a piece of white paper over a section of the trunk and rub the surface with a soft pencil or crayon.

When drawing a tree, sketch the overall shape first before you draw in the detail. Fill a whole piece of paper with your tree shape to make it really dramatic!

1 Lightly sketch in the trunk and the overall outline of the tree.

2 Draw the main branches, making them thinner at the ends.

3 Add fine lines for the smaller twigs, right up to the edge of the outline.

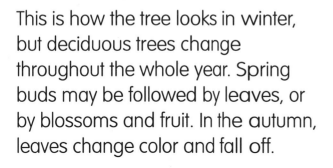

This is how the tree looks in winter, but deciduous trees change throughout the whole year. Spring buds may be followed by leaves, or by blossoms and fruit. In the autumn, leaves change color and fall off.

Soft pencils or charcoal are ideal for drawing wintry trees. For a dramatic effect, use white chalk on black paper. Just color the spaces around the tree, and in between the branches, to make a unique and dramatic silhouette.

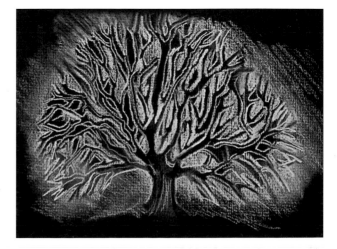

Cityscapes

A cityscape is a view of a city. Don't worry that buildings are too complicated to draw—the trick is to look at everything carefully and to build up the picture from patterns and shapes.

1 Decide what you are going to put into your picture. Are there any interesting buildings in your area? Use your viewfinder (page 23) to help you decide which is the best view. You could also use a scene from a postcard or a book.

2 First, draw the outlines on a wide piece of paper. Look carefully at the buildings—are they wider than they are tall? Do the roofs slope steeply, or are they flat?

3 When you have done the outlines, sketch in the doors and windows. Note how big they are compared to the rest of the building.

4 Add the other details, such as chimneys, spires, porches, steps, stones, wood, and brick patterns. Finish by adding color, using white to create highlights for bright spots.

Build your own

To make a building look three-dimensional, you need to show its side view in addition to its front.

1 Draw the front of the building.

2 Draw in the sides, to make a cube.

3 Add a roof, door, and windows.

4 Shade the side of the house lightly. Add a shadow on the ground if you want to make it even more realistic.

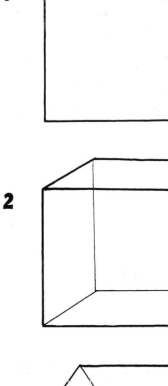

1

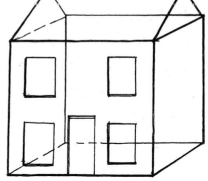

2

3

4

Using a grid

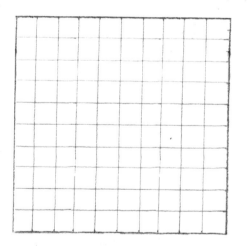

Drawing is about looking and copying what you see. Sometimes our mind tricks us, and we draw what we expect to see, not what is actually in front of us. Using a grid can help you get the **proportions** exactly right and can also help you make your pictures larger or smaller.

1 Take a photo or magazine cutting, and trace the outline of the picture you want to copy onto tracing paper. Now divide your tracing into equal squares, using a ruler to help you.

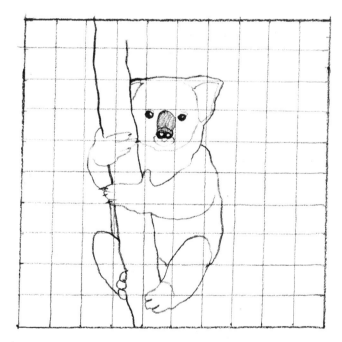

2 Take a sheet of paper and make the same number of squares using a soft pencil. You can make the squares the same size as the ones on the tracing paper, or they can be smaller or bigger.

3 Copy the main outlines of the picture into each square, one by one. Concentrate on one square at a time, rather than looking at the whole picture.

Upside-down drawing

Choose a picture from a magazine, and draw a grid over it, making sure the grid is visible from the back side of the picture. Turn the picture upside down. Make another grid on a sheet of white paper. Try to copy what you can see in each square, including all the shading. The end result may be more accurate in some ways, because you are focusing on color and shade, rather than trying to draw the details.

Using a posterboard or an oversized sheet of paper, make a big poster of an animal for your wall. Use the grid technique with chalks or charcoals to fill in large areas quickly.

4 When the main outline is complete, erase the guidelines and fill in the smaller details, using the photo as a guide.

Glossary

background the area in the back of a picture, behind the main object

chalk a soft, dusty material used for making soft, smudgy pictures

charcoal a dark gray drawing material made from charred wood

construction paper a rough-textured paper—good for chalk and charcoal drawings

highlights the lightest parts of a image, used to show the shinyness of a surface, or the place where light is most concentrated

horizontal from side to side

landscape an outdoor scene, such as a country scene with trees and hills, or an urban scene with factories and buildings

outlines the lines that form the outer edges of the objects of your picture. You usually draw these first and add the details later.

portfolio a case for storing and carrying your drawings

proportion the size of one thing or group of things compared to the size of another thing or group of things

shading darker areas of color added to a picture

silhouette a drawing of an object that is filled in with a dark color so that you only see its shape, not details such as color or texture

sketch paper very smooth paper, good for making final drawings

texture the surface of something. Some paper has a smooth texture, others have a rougher texture.

vertical up and down

Index

Notes for parents and teachers

The projects in this book can be used as stand-alone art projects or as part of other areas of study, such as science or geography. While the ideas in the book are offered as inspiration, children should always be encouraged to draw from their imagination and first-hand observation.

Sourcing ideas

All art projects should tap into children's interests and be relevant to their lives and experiences. Some stimulating starting points include found objects, discussions about their family and pets, hobbies, TV shows, or favorite places.

Encourage children to source their own ideas and references, from books, magazines, or the Internet. Digital cameras are a great means of documenting references (pictures of landscapes, people, or animals) that can be printed out later to look at while drawing.

Other lessons can often be an ideal springboard for an art project—for example, a science field trip can lead to a collection of bark rubbings and leaves, which could serve as a starting point for drawing a landscape.

Encourage children to keep a sketchbook of their ideas, and to collect other images and objects to help them develop their drawings.

Give children as many first-hand experiences as possible through visits and contact with creative people.

Evaluating work

It's important and motivating for children to share their work with others, and to compare ideas and methods. Encourage them to talk about their work. What do they like best about it? How would they do it differently next time?

Show the children examples of other artists' work. How did they tackle the same subject and problems? Do the children like the work? Why or why not?

Help children to recognize the originality and value of their work, to appreciate the different qualities in others' work, and to respect ways of working that are different from their own. Display children's work for all to admire!

Going further

Look at ways to develop extensions to a project. For example, many of the ideas in this book could be used in conjunction with painting, collage, and print-making. You could use image-enhancing computer software and digital scanners to build up and juxtapose images.

Help your artist(s) set up an art gallery to show off their work, or scan artwork and post the images to a photo website where others can log in and view them. Having their work displayed professionally will make them feel that their work is valued.